some words suicidal

Stella Vinitchi Radulescu

Červená Barva Press
Somerville, Massachusetts

Červená Barva Press
P.O. Box 440357
W. Somerville, MA 02144-3222

www.cervenabarvapress.com

Bookstore: www.thelostbookshelf.com

Cover Art: *Icône en confidence* by Michel Bénard

Cover Design: William J. Kelle

Production: Christian Mailloux and Mikail Jaikaran

ISBN: 978-0-9861111-1-2

Distributed by Small Press Distribution: www.spdbooks.org

Acknowledgments

My thanks to the editors of the following publications where these poems first appeared:

Asheville Poetry Review: "Nostalgia"
Sixth Finch: "Some Words Suicidal"
Wallace Stevens Journal: "Chicago and the Rest of the World Watching the Moon"
Symmetry Pebbles: "Paris in Sepia," "Lovers in Winter"
Red Booth Review: "Coffee so Far"
Yew Journal: "Plainsong," "Our Heaven"
Thoughtsmith Review: "Romanian Ghetto," "Writing the Circle"
Emerge Literary Journal: "The Origin of Music"
Inertia Magazine: "Tea Time in Heaven"
Gris-Gris Journal of Literature: "April Fever"
Josephine Quarterly: "Renaissance," "Pastoral View"

Table of Contents

1. Pastoral View

2. Getting There

I, of whom I know nothing, I know my eyes are open, because of the tears that pour from them unceasingly.

I invented love, music, the smell of flowering currant, to escape from me.

— Samuel Beckett, *The Unnamable*

some words suicidal

one

pastoral view

SHORT ENCOUNTER

Made in the air
by the air the Hour   / bring your

shovel to bury me in its shade /
narrow as it is the window

doesn't allow the view to shine
the wing

to fly   we need more roses
and then more words

to call them such

listen

the noise the bleating of the stars
who wants

to carry the world—

/ who cut us off from the answer /

RENAISSANCE

Flying is a matter of style

silence will strap you on Earth

the Renaissance gardens won't fit
in your eyes

But remember

you are still a clod in my hands
I can mold you

again

*

The skylark took off—

the blue grew higher the world grew deeper

one can see the bottom of the day
migrating

Mother, how I fear you now your huge eye
from which soon

Winter will come

RECURRING DAYS

Winter party and the mind sinks
in wonder
the moving sand ahead and

elsewhere:
I don't miss you today as I don't miss
the world

spreading around like amnesia   the tree
the sun
and inside out

recurring days
sleepwalkers on the roof

I trust you light even though the bluebird

has changed
to black

it takes a song—
here comes another color another sound

memory

white

I hear wolves upstairs in the attic

ODE TO A SWAN OR TO IMAGINATION

Swan of the last man
imagining *a man*—

like you
floating in dense air snow wings

snow mind it's hard
not to think

not to love what really is
or isn't

the naked hand the body mirroring
its absence

the blue regresses to life—
days after

and days before
I woke up as a song

NIGHT RAIN

The world is wet from last night's rain

the candle won't burn

so why are you waiting it takes centuries

it takes lives weeks

seconds

to get

that fragrance back in the air—you may not see

the end   *the clock slows down*

the rose explodes

a hand moves farther

sign after sign

I choose not to blink

PHILOSOPHER OF CHAIRS CLOUDS EGGS

I see a chair he said
the brain
philosopher of clouds chairs eggs

just at the time when flying
upside down
it was dissolving
in particles
of light

Should I continue or just die—

Or you can touch it
with your tongue he said in all
the languages

I know—
I tried to get it back in place in fact
in time

around my disappearing table

SOME WORDS SUICIDAL

...arithmetic leads to philology, and philology leads to crime...
—Eugène Ionesco

If you are still playing on the ground
still dreaming of a long
blue sentence
you may be using the word *sand* or talk
about your sister
your friends
little hands building the square face

of the moon
or want to jump
or say good-bye childhood too long
my hair grew wild
until it reached
the end
another danger *time*

and flying back don't dare to open
your mouth
you'll be swallowed up by hungry sounds
the rope too short
the sky too far
if you say *this* or *that* you might be burnt alive
your ashes

already here beware
of the word *now*

THE ORIGIN OF MUSIC

> " *Things as they are*
> *Are changed upon the blue guitar.* "
> —Wallace Stevens

Light comes from the rear window except Sunday morning—

too far too cold

and the craving to write about things

things as they are

saliva as a sign

an image leaves the body

where are the clouds—

the baby sucks   milk spilled over the page

small mounds of earth   *o night o music*

the nipples suck back:

                    no punctuation

mammals with wings

if you dare

LOVERS IN WINTER

Black waves are Winter waves
the green came later
with a splash

of light

our eyes bigger & bigger   we were
lovers in Winter growing
young

with the wind

We are humans in Spring   pink
and blue bodies
streets turning to dreams—

Stay tuned

colors may change   God was
off-white
now

poisonous red

RELATIVITY

You stood still but the hummingbird

in your eyes

addicted you to speed

the speed of light   the growing

distance to the moon

minus your night   what remains

makes no difference

: you keep moving

IMITATION OF A MAN SO HE WILL NEVER FAIL

He sits in the Museum of Rain

triangular made out of small gestures

sand

flesh & spirit a crack

in the stone captive like God

in his own name   resembling

a ghost

the meaning itself—

/ my dog reads Dante and gnaws

the bones /

The king the analyst sexologist of Time

stuck among umbrellas

and mice

a man of honor honoring

the dust—

I step aside

I go by days I go by numbers and silence his tongue

NUDE IN THE SNOW

The flesh starts with a song
snow starts late night talking of white—

somewhere a wound

: the goddess with no arms and human scar
instead

the bleeding rose

the garden

*

The moon has dragged the body behind
your eyes

the nude not really nude

the difference is time

what you should see   the healing   white
melting

in your mouth   the flame
loosing power

in flashing sounds

AND THEN THERE IS MATISSE

And then there is Matisse I would like to write about

visiting the museum of men hanging up

to a cloud   women

go straight to red

which is blue at times

and what if I fail to show my face as beautiful as it is

painted in aquarelle   the scarf

the burning eyes

in the mirror

I am an obscure sign and I can't move

WHAT REMAINS

She is my mother still alive
and well in my late Winter
sleep

her talking mute   mute
as a dream

a silenced tongue
is worth the rhyme
smoke goes upstairs and

into the sky :
I deserted you one Summer
afternoon

when comets like children
were playing around
but eyes and flesh :

your eyes your flesh on the page
I am reaching your hand   you have dropped
mine

PUPPET HEART

Puppet heart there are some words for you
in the closet

 a silky robe the moon—

Tell me the hour tell me whose eyes
not mine

How do I feel

Emerald is a stone   blood is for human use—
blood prints in the snow

you must be the spy

ssssh...   somebody sleeps

I should not call or call you beast hippopotamus
twin stars

Cassiopeia

the stage is empty   people come & go
bonjour bonsoir

there is a hole never a whole

Today I am wearing the Earth tomorrow the Sky

here are the strings   you are the player

I am the fool

pure death

CONFESSION

To write is hard and the day goes by—
I didn't water the plants
the country I was born went up in flames

Is four a number the greasy tongue of the clock
the size of the room
the year to come?

That's it   I shouldn't ask
more dust on the floor the vacuum
roars

messages keep coming like birds that lost
their voice
the sky is black (I may go back to the first line

and dedicate this to you)

Turn on the news
open the windows there are clothes to dry clean
there are dreams to dream:

You got used to cold weather I got used to flames
the ink spills over the page still raining still Monday—

Love is a fish to catch with empty hands

PASTORAL VIEW

The trail gets loose in cold imagination

loose

losing

lost

the cock-a-doodle-do the egg the panoramic view—

but leaves were real little tombs and warm

the day under my feet

must have been

Spring

I said tomorrow

you said yesterday

trees rising to the sky like candles   lips

that take the shape

of the moon

A COW IN HEAVEN PLAYING THE BLUES

It came to this: the living
and the dead

after the song the pretty day
with pretty cows

in black & white scattered
in time

and grazing light—one more
thought

for you my friend unseen
unborn

and playing chess with kings
& rats

two

getting there

THESE WORDS ARE BEES STARS ANTS

These words are bees are stars are ants roaming
on the page

beyond understanding

*

or the absurdity of footprints

*

I faked my face but it came back
in thousands of beautiful
deaths

the illiterate soul   sounds falling
like snow
on closed eyes

THE WIND WILL TELL (1)

The sea like Mozart writes a symphony

for people longtime gone

they gather up & down and nothing

in the middle

that's maybe true

big eyes big ears sometimes a pause

a broken string

or maybe silence plays the violin

in purple chambers the wind will tell

the gathering at dusk

waves to the ceiling

they need more rooms they need more chairs

an infinite

SPRING ON THE GROUND YELLOW SUNGLASSES

Spring on the ground yellow sunglasses—

yellow little souls pushing up

dandelions & all

as if Rimbaud had lost some of his vowels

and being around

sits on the bench flows in the air

more sounds

less colors

waves come in pairs

sun comes in rhymes   could be the same

Then?   Now?   Or ever?

He doesn't care

PLAINSONG

If you are here
in front
of the door
you are the time
the story
to be told
your trembling
lips and
Heaven
slipping through
your words
dead
or alive
the heart gives
back
the gift
of life
the shiver goes
to bones
and
wanes in flesh
your sleep
or our sleepy
waters—
the wrong moon
rises
over the plains

AKHMATOVA AT THE DOOR

If enjoying light dark sits at the bottom

bare arms dark souls   nobody

tells us where to go imagine a century

of snow

all the phones ringing

Akhmatova at the door

I was holding the letter I was wearing

black boots—*would you trade*

your words your eyes you hair—

while passing the river a coin

in my mouth

Death scarves for sale.

mix & match

and a free corpse

CREATION

1.

The first sentence comes as a gift darkness and light

melted in a bucket

Then comes the angel

and sits on the chair don't move

I said

moving my head in the right direction

2.

Such distraction   the balloonist

the ascension

the flying

but dogs don't fly and this is an example of

how useless is a wing on paper

or a paper wing

BEYOND THE BLACK FENCE

The music tickles the roof
in the garden beyond the black fence
they are trying to find
a way out

she climbs a tiny shadow
that circles the oak
he knocks at the invisible door
between purple
and red

there is a mist in the air like sweat
desolation comes in fine
steps
searching for the grass

they can't touch while shameless
gestures of life
are pouring around
with the rain

PARIS IN SEPIA

It's like a beat in my head

cold weather and soupe gratinée

once in a while a poet throws

himself into eternal

life

the Seine takes his body –

RED

I am waiting for the Summer to come

and for you to read my poems

the eye blinks

a hand moves the sun to the left

words like these damage the page

wind blows time blows

the truth—

as the knife approaches

arteries & veins

A LEAF OF GRASS

A leaf of grass red blue or green—

this is how Spring starts how eyes

get used to light

the sky the music of the lake

the Master died in pain blindness

for Joy

night for the day

listen to the wind   somewhere

the grass keeps growing red

IMAGINE THE WIND

Imagine the wind
your face in the wind
your hair
your life your corpse
like a sailboat like a floating
scarecrow

the window you could never
reach from outside
now at your feet broken
to pieces
imagine the wind
tickling

the sand
one by one the white
translucent gravel of your
life
small tiny bodies shifted
by time

never again a window

GETTING THERE

Getting there
finding the spot
      never called time

tiptoeing your life
on a ghostly street getting
      there—

          there is only one language
          you as a tree your arms
          branches
               growing
                    around

birds will come
light will shine
      and the wind
      will take you back
          to your
               full desire

LANDSCAPE & MORE

To paint a heart you need some red an oval
or a square
men with golden teeth golden hair sitting on the bench
reading Voltaire

Jardin du Luxembourg would be ideal   I come and go
with my spring look
I used to like the weather the timing

Remember...

The sun came down it was too late sleepy
the swans
your wooden face
I left the painting on the grass

I left it blank

INTIMACY

Late afternoon coming again
they come and pass
late birds
from undisclosed

skies
you move your chair next
to mine
between us

a breeze of time

how do I look? — naked
framed hanging
on the wall
a glass of wine in one hand

bread in the other   : what has
to be grasped
what has to be said

I use the monster trick and pass the Styx

LOVE POEM

We hardly knew each other still this is for you

I closed the door

put down the cigarette

the ash

the truth about living   some music

it breaks my heart

we barely talked however we learned things

from each other

things about clouds about wind

you take my hand I imagine—

we step to the day

sit on the grass

there is no age there is no time

I learned not to love you

and watching the oak the last leaf is falling

OVER THE BRIDGE

Thoughts are big roaming at night
they don't sleep
some do things like cutting the grass taking
out the trash

flying over the Pacific some are allergic to life
afraid to go downstairs
or take a knife

deep roots under the bed
masquées
and wearing clocks and wigs
my pillow flows down
the river—

I stand for peace and for a hot shower
all the way struggling
with a white
flower

he loves me he loves me not   become a face

a virgin a mother keep tolling
the hour

THE ASSUMPTION OF SUMMER

1.

Cold feet the war so far do you understand
this language
the way it swings from day to night the way
it litters   here comes

again our sweet Planet   a destiny of silence
no stars   vowels collapsing
at dawn

2.

I saw them on TV the rodents the ladies the kings
the new generation of rats tearing apart
the screen

Mademoiselle knows how to fit the day into night
and walks at sundown
on high heals

one step ahead and closer to a word she doesn't want to say

three

today   as if

REAR VIEW FROM A FRESH GRAVE

She keeps hiding her face. She moves
and moves the stone

with her ivory hands.

You or her. Running under
the sea

short sleeves
silky hair let's memorize the day the food

the color of the earth.

        The big question of Who—

SPRING LETTERS

1.
The sidewalk ends in weeds and grief

we are on the road

wearing high boots waterproof hearts

slim like ghosts

we step

aside

the stormy bells are telling all

2.
I put together two strong winds

and cut in pieces

dreams

the smoke got to the roof like blood

your letter says

it's Spring

3.
There is a highway with no name

between dusty days   small lives wrapped up

in sounds

the bluebird digs the air eternity

makes loops—

the sculpture comes to life   : the art

of thinking blue

SLOW SONG

I imagine myself sitting on the porch writing this letter

to you

moonlight and all—

as if nothing had happened to us both on the same side

of the hour

the pen in my right hand   a slight inclination

of the Planet

slides down the paper   : it came so close to your eyes almost

inside the frame

the language I was using never again the same

RÉSUMÉ

One full eye rolling in vain   more than

you expect   a body of work

forthcoming from the press

four legs and I give two

to a friend

If you could walk where would you go

Millions of cells coming together make me think:

I promised you the story with no end

the rage of words

me caught in dementia

and skipping turns like burying stars

If you could say something what would you say

METROPOLIS

Like water dripping down the wall

nuit nuit notte noapte   terrestrial
language for aliens

their big tongues at the door

it's Winter
forget the time the guillotine

look for me in the basement the red
building

on 55th street   I'll be playing
the trumpet

or already did—music and stones
the concierge

in black & white like a myth
dangles the bell

Says no

TODAY   AS IF

Today—

as if yesterday never existed
or would exist
as if someone cried and I didn't listen or I had dead eyes
or a myriad
as if plains and oceans had been swept along with the weather—

today—
a swell a mound
on the hot planet / that desolation /   umbilical time
look at me
my red shirt

the picture in four nails   and Winter on the road

another heart is set up for tomorrow

THE WIND WILL TELL (2)

The raven ravening the place

as ravens are the visionaries

machines in time

sound after sound

a rosary:

they take us to a prayer

clock down clock up

the air is ticking

Spring time in Portugal

snow drifts in Heaven

humans are not allowed

: such clarity

CREATIVE WRITING

the cell phone rings but it's in vain

technology that fails when

everything turns white, the bad dream

of a fly—

I don't remember when it started

the decay of my teeth   melancholy   like

Roman Empire

we must have been hungry

looking through the window   the planetary life—

I don't buy cooked shrimps

you said

I buy them raw, and guns with memory

the trigger

upside down

COUNTING OUT

Go wild go crazy go broke
one tooth
one eye
for everything around

much to do isn't worth to be done   *He* was asleep
when I was born
so I pulled myself out of the dark

the skull ahead
what a joy

the rhyme sticks on my tongue   I discovered
the clock I discovered

the sun   Godless blue   : you can come

DAYS AND FIREFLIES

> *"There are no days here, but I use the expression."*
> —Samuel Beckett

climbing the hour our new sun

days and fireflies

all knowledge all ruling

                    Let's talk -

(in words like these)

the hawk has eaten the liver I invite you to the feast

of our time

you might come as a child

or father

and turn off the light

OUR HEAVEN

Our Heaven

our dogs eat from

the same

evening pot where

the sky dumps

a full bag

of stars

I have this vision

of all the visions

at once:

sentimental

like the moon

I ride the hills

and delete

the return

RECEDING LIGHT

Follow your shadow to the nearest town
sit down

watch
does it shine does it remember your body

the shape the heaviness over the years one name
or another

I may drag my thoughts from the pond
the light recedes

the case about existing

I inherited some words they crack at the edge—

move your feet

*

Vallejo's heralds fell to the ground

NOVEMBER FLIES WITH ASHES

The Earth opens its crypts there is hope
there is still hope for everyone who honors
the place with less than
a breath

November flies with ashes from soul
to soul
in the story I write lingering on the page
imagining the snow

geese are gone
seven hills to the top   I stumble
like God—
to shop for Heaven it takes your life

skim milk on my list the clock the flooding
the tolling
I'm getting used to things   The Grand Design—
I am in

holding on each & every duck
yellow my dress

ducking time

I'll be waiting
for another round

Who said that

DEATH ON THE BALCONY

The two the four the five the forever—

metaphysics of numbers

the flag   cheap love
the language of the poor

language of

blind

*

The unexpected season   Spring—
forgotten bodies on the roof

Death on the balcony

and growing deep and growing old

in the mirror   I already saw my face:
the melody of snow falling

on empty lots

WAR FACE

I saw it smiling I saw it blue
and crying

who lost a leg an arm should praise the sun—
louder the voice

smaller a life

the cock keeps crowing the day keeps coming:

it's called nostalgia the old obsession
with colors and sounds

while living—the fabric shrinks   not
to compare to other things like plastic birds

& plastic stars   the TV on   I shiver:
so much to die so many times

a war at home
another coming and all the tears all the excitement

I wish
to be in the middle

I wish to be at large
I wish to be buried with my boots on

a holy scene with puppets and guns
no more dreams

nobody sleeps

FLOOD

You are not alone and you are alone under the lonely sky
With your glory in your back-pack wrapped with your shirt
And your shoes
With the world shrinking in your throat.

You are not alone and you are alone with your few words frozen
In your heart, the light frozen in your eyes.
An invisible hand moves the Queen
From white to black...
And the sky breaks on your shoulders.

You are alone and you are not alone in your death,
Stars are watching you. We will take your back-pack home
Along with your glory.

Evening comes too early, windows are shattered by strange winds.

We are waiting, still waiting for you here, around the table.
We can't sleep or cook dinner tonight, your blood

has flooded the sink.

INTRUSIVE

Waves on my pillow sweating

the cloud

the knife on the floor   slaughter

at dawn

your hunger flooded the room

                : expect long delays

for my name to go back to the body it takes the sun

the spider the dreary meal the coffee

one full cup

GLOVES ON THE TABLE

The clock was sick
I was in bed

the coffee brewing
the Winter

slowing
gloves on the table

going West
winds

filthy sheets and
the tumor

night in my chest
how about

lightning
words can do it

would you mind beauty
won't last

skip the rest the
forever

look for my name
under the lost name

of God

SNOW IN THE FORECAST

Days come   gloomy days   the wounds won't heal

words won't shine

people on my street are walking

their dogs

some too thin some too fat in shorts in wheelchairs

in an arctic mood

some jogging some crawling, the repentant ones,

and those from last spring and those

who don't belong to us

they went broke

they have reached a higher zone   cold

in their mouths more silence

than sounds

pages go fast   days come when everybody

wears white

tonight it's going to snow

four

lonely angels

IT WAS YESTERDAY

I was walking
neither on Earth nor in the sky
empty eyes fullness
in one hand
don't touch me said a voice touching
my lips

—as in a coma
pale & more pale the lady
with hollow face
enlightens us
again—heat was coming

from old snow
a melting tongue oh, Come on girl
don't leave me now or lose
your hair

the next day it was yesterday   the sin
the Art of not being

bare foot I stepped on the grass already a dream

FLAMINGO SCENE

It has a sharp appearance among brothers

and sisters the sound

of the sea

the color of wind

Time rushed to my window your statue there

your beak

scooping late night dreams

bottom of sleep

half mud

half music

      And dumping suns and rolling vowels:

the scream came clear as water

the Thing called death   the world

on one leg

APRIL FEVER

Let's sit down & chat   the last two chairs

of the season start moving

backwards   let's hold hands & go crazy

about each other's eyes

while under our feet something final

something big echoes   desire

and loss

the midnight song of the Earth

the roaming stars

Let's be silent sitting there like two frozen angels

in the Square   Come   come you rose

that bled in my eyes before night

before the freeze

before everything

Let the world go on let the Spring come

NOSTALGIA

What is returning?
Nearly nothing, but it could be a flake of snow.
—Paul Celan

If I am getting somewhere it would be
a place like this
that fits
in the moon   solid light

an apple
a skull wrapped up in jasmine fragrance
once I was a fish
in your friendly eye

after all we are not the same nor
different
from our gods flowering yellow or blue

in the yard   we are supposed
to be the guests—

if I am getting nowhere it would be
a place that fits in your mind
a very long sentence

or simply
a word   if I called it wind
it would roar

SECRET SOULS

In & out up & down finally

here. Where I was.

Before.

Before knowing or being. Finally the flame

the fire that built the fire.

The urgency of *yes*.

Let's not talk in tongues.

Let's not be saved.

The body flip-flops.

Clouds on top.

Maybe a soul.

CHICAGO AND THE REST OF THE WORLD WATCHING THE MOON

The moon is the mother of pathos and pity.
—Wallace Stevens

Chicago and the rest of the world watching

the moon

the whaling the sailing the glitter

thousands of years ago lost

in the thicket—

theme & conclusion as we talk

and vanish

in our own words   a poet thinks it's time

to shower & shave

time to sit down and write a moonlight sonnet

COFFEE SO FAR

Coffee so far   a hand rolling time
like a thick Russian
cigar

fingers move along a wooden table but

in another version stillness was the word
of the month

August—
do angels smell like tears?

IN TRENCHES THE LENGH OF POETRY LINES

In trenches the length of poetry lines
it was water and cold

later on came the rats
my grandfather was looking for his hat

he also lost a house a country and a wife
hope & bread coming in a big truck

let's kill the driver
and lay down the corpse

between these letters closing the gap

MATERNITY

Are you from where I should leave—years crumbling
in my hands like old pages

are you coming in my direction—winds have shifted it
from East

to nowhere
or maybe you have missed the turn and now—where

are you now pale like the moon carrying the child
at your breast

SHARING

We share the air sometimes the bed

the orchid's sweet rainfall

inflorescence—

half sun moon half waiting for each other

the mystery of Summer

the refrain

growing into dirt   words grow

into silence

the daily game of *nevermore*—

Be a bee my destiny   I am not mortal

WRITING TAKES MORE THAN BERRYMAN' S BEARD

It was at night when I discovered
the ghost tiptoeing in the house
the floor
the carpet decorated
with national
feelings

the anthem in vivid colors—
we were sitting outside
in the open world
so Henry
could find himself alive

rather good food *chicken paprika*
than art - *the original crime*
nobody saw us our bones dis-
appearing

don't we have the right
to make love on the other side
of the bed
down to a single word
down
to the river

LONELY ANGELS

They play on the street
and die by the lake

a song on its way
to the sky

we let them in
we feed them   milk

& blood
old stories—they smile

the music gets on top—

fear them all

said Rilke when they come

too close

to your heart

THE BLIND LADY ON ADAM STREET

The air I breathe so clear   I see my arms
my body
in the mirror past sleeping clouds and sleeping
birds

the breathing time

my fantasy *is creeping up*   could this cold air
have come from one of Stevens' lines?

The city moves and moving it gets to the next
stop
men travel in pairs women by train

and the pigeons on Oak Beach and Russian
Tea Time the bar   that is that
the pitching time

Am I the blind—
the blind lady begging on Adam Street
Chicago.com?

I skip the present

A century for a buck

READING PROUST

As I write to you news from above keep coming
flooding the town I mean every silky
deadly night

you know how much I want to be with you
in a place like this
a body of hours under the stars

infinity—

fathers I heard go to war while mothers
read Proust

: a memory deal

        I tore apart the picture
        you left
        on the shelf as a sign of your disappearance

ROMANIAN GHETTO

I live in the ghetto
and play the balalaïka
and that's not all
if you call me a man
I won't answer
I was supposed to play
the banjo
and to be called
God

*

walls are built to be torn down
hands to be free
free to peel potatoes
to make potato soup

or else
the children came to the window
hunger & sweat in their eyes

whose children

what soup

*

I breathe your breath but you don't know—
don't know what happened
when we passed the bridge   bang
bang
the hour far away and I can't see the end

you on the other side—
we took off our shoes switched lines

and then

MALAISE

The sister I don't have starts
drinking my blood

The man I don't love keeps
coming into my dream

Strangely true these roses
of death

Like truth itself

A poet dying seeks refuge and
sets the page on fire

TEA TIME IN HEAVEN

we painted the room
in black

silverware on the table
black cups black

hands
ready to grasp

we painted some birds
on our plates

and then
we ate them

alive

THE AFTERLIFE

: a life
like this walking at noon on the street
a woman   her hat yellow
green or blue

the pungent red sometimes
the roof—
downstairs the rotten apples
on the shelf

aligned in circle or in pairs the peeling
went too fast   too deep—
the seeds like women after love
closing their eyes

the house collapsed   so late it was

It was so far

EMERALD SONG

I am here   so many
for so long

the prisoner in nobody's prison   his ear
tuned to the sound

of my name—two in one
one can imagine

the all time Time
the all time Speech   no words no leaves

no waves—that mist behind things
suppose

you are taking my name   the assassin in his erotic
mood

is rolling up his sleeves

THE YELLOW TAKES ME HOME

A lane of Yellow led the eye
Unto a Purple Wood...
    —Emily Dickinson

The yellow takes me home November dream
in the deserted
town

the threshold farther than I thought my mother
thinner than the day
I left

almost invisible and almost dead she spoke
she speaks—her voice
in yellow tones

I might have been carried away with the leaves

ENDING LINE

A speeding heart   the ending line
bridges
and cherry trees in blossom   *I used to be*

To play to die
an open field   a pantomime

Things out of grasp and things I touched
consider the eyes

                      the face...

the lonely face the snowy eyes

What makes you think

I'm alive

WRITING THE CIRCLE

At least it's closed. The door. Between
going & going.
Like a butterfly the thought sits
on white. Bien bien. Some colors. The geometry.

Humiliation of space.
My voice doesn't know how to be a voice.
Or a drop of rain.
We are not made to cry. It takes place. Now.

Poetry time is what I mean. From my room.
From the heart.
Want to add a star a vowel some water
a giraffe? Between going & going.

What remains.
Do not carry your books your children your past.
Leaving. Lifting the ban on dreams. Pretty clear.
The reptile's eye is watching.

Rain. Fire. Fire and rain. Your Majesty you are blind
or dead.
May I have your umbrella?
And the answer was yes.

ABOUT THE AUTHOR

Stella Vinitchi Radulescu, Ph.D. in French Language & Literature, is the author of numerous collections of poetry published in the United States, Romania and France. She writes poetry in English, French and Romanian and her poems have appeared in *Laurel Review*, *Asheville Poetry Review*, *Wallace Stevens Journal*, *Seneca Review*, *Pleiades*, *Rhino*, *Louisville Review* among others, as well as in a variety of literary magazines in France, Belgium, Luxembourg, Québec and Romania. She is the winner of several International Poetry Prizes awarded for her French books, including the Prix Amélie Murat (2013) and the Grand Prix de la Francophonie (2014). A collection of her *New & Selected Poems* is forthcoming from Orison Books Press. At the present she lives in Chicago.